Unfaded Beauty

by

Karen Y. Ranney

Volume I

The New Proverbs 31 Woman Series

Unfaded Beauty

by

Karen Y. Ranney

"*A blessed book! This is a very good teaching and much needed in the Body of Christ. My Sister in Christ, Dr. Karen Ranney, speaks volumes of big truth in this one little book. She backs it all up with God's uncompromised Word and somehow wraps it all in His incredible love for humanity.*

"*I was not surprised she wrote on this subject so well, as I have watched her, and her husband, embrace God's love and walk in His Truth; as well as teach and demonstrate them to others everywhere they travel.*

"*I believe we've not yet seen this wonderful couples' teaching ministry in full manifestation—but it's coming.*"

Aaron D, Jones, Author of 8 books
Christian Publisher
Evangelist and Missionary

Dedication

This book would never have been written without the Holy Spirit prompting me so strongly. I praise God for giving me this opportunity to share my heart and His heart with women. My main inspiration has come from my precious mother, Elwanda McMinn. Mom taught me the Word of God as a child and led by her example of a godly, holy life. She is a prayer warrior and has shared with me, through prayer and counsel, in the making of this book. Thank you, mom!

My husband, Allen Ranney, has also been a great inspiration in the writing of this book. He has been a sounding board for my thoughts, that have sometimes been quite lengthy…bless His dear heart for being patient and helping me in the writing of this book.

~ Karen Y. Ranney

Table of Contents

Foreword

When I first heard my wife, Karen, speaking about how her heart ached for women because of the lies they've been spoon-fed since they were babies, I had to stop and ask her what she was talking about. Karen then began to explain because women do not know God's love and affirmation of them, society, with its ever-changing standards, conformity and competition has done a great disservice to women all over the world, especially in the western world, Europe, and America.

Imposing on them immoral standards of dress, speech, and behavior under the guise of progressive modern thinking. Deceiving them to believe that the new "best thing", "fad" or "rage" in clothing or outward accessories will make them happy. Modesty being thrown out the window as antiquated. Chastity, purity, holiness, and righteousness mocked by an ever-increasing sinful culture.

I asked what could be done? What should be done?

Karen explained that she had a book in her heart about how God wants to have a close love relationship with women which will cause them (by showing them His love, affirmation, and acceptance) to want to please the Lord with a godly lifestyle. It would help them to seek after holiness and righteousness in every area of their lives. I thought wow! If there is a lady qualified to write that book it would be Karen, as she was raised with sound biblical teaching, her father being a pastor, and she has a personal, close relationship with Jesus and loves to read/study the Word of God.

Karen lays a firm scriptural foundation for every statement in this book and by the time you finish reading, you will understand she is that Proverbs 31 woman and you are well on your way to become the next.

Brace yourself and prepare your heart, mind, and spirit to receive what God is telling women about His desire for an intimate relationship with them and how this will affect how they act, dress and speak.

Proverbs 12:4
"A virtuous woman is a crown to her husband: but she that makes ashamed is as rottenness in his bones."

Shalom,
Allen C. Ranney Th. D

Author's Preface

The reason these books are being written is I have felt compelled by God, as a Christian woman, to care for other women's needs and concerns. This has been on my heart for quite some time. Because of struggles in my own life as a woman, my heart goes out to women who struggle with low self-esteem, tormenting thoughts, lack of real peace, feeling in competition and comparison with other women. This has caused me to cry out to God and to study His Word regarding the needs of women everywhere. God's heart breaks and so does mine with how the enemy of our souls has brought such torment into our hearts that does not have to be there.

In the book of Titus 2:3-5 it says *"The aged women likewise, that they be in behavior as becomes holiness, not false accusers, not given to much wine, teachers of good things; That they may teach the young women to be sober, to love their husbands, to love their children, To be discreet, chaste, keepers at home, good, obedient to their own husbands, that the Word of God be not blasphemed."*

I may not be an aged woman, at least I hope I don't look like one, ha, ha, but I have been a Christian since I was a girl, nine years old, about 50 years ago. I have struggled in many of the areas that I would like to address in this book. My heart goes out to women everywhere who struggle in these same areas. Even though I was raised as a Pastor's kid and heard and learned many things from the Bible, I still struggled with understanding how much God loves me and how precious and beautiful I am in His eyes. It seems like I could not understand the will of God for my life as a Christian woman. I struggled with being able to rightly divide the Word. I also struggled with trying to understand what legalism was or what was pleasing to God.

I'm sure that there are many women who will read this that have the same or similar struggles. Since God has given me more understanding of the whole picture in the last few years and what His heart is, I would like to share this with as many women as possible. If I can help even one woman not to struggle the way I have in my life it will be worth it all. After much prayer and contemplation seeking the Lord's face, this is what I believe He wants me to share from His Word and His heart. I pray it will be a very encouraging exhortation and a help to each and every one that reads this series.

In Christ,
Karen Y. Ranney

Introduction

I have enjoyed writing this book knowing that my Heavenly Father delighted in downloading this into my heart to share with my dear sisters in Christ.

We, as women, seem to have an insatiable desire to be beautiful. I know, I have. It seems to drive us and cause us to be discontented, always searching for affirmation, praise, and even love from others. The world comes to us in our weakness and torments us, tempting us to conform to others and their opinions.

My struggle in understanding God's love and acceptance of me has caused me to want to help my sisters in Christ find this freedom that only a close relationship with Jesus can bring.

What issues are you, dear sister, struggling with in your life? Are you searching for an everlasting love, true affirmation and/or praise that will build you up and make you whole?

This book is about helping us to see Jesus's face and to understand His deep everlasting love, gentleness, tender mercies and loving kindness to us as women. It is to help us seek Christ's face and to know His great love that desires us to be made whole in Him. To know the love of Christ that surpasses all understanding, to know His perfect love that casts out all fear and to be set free to live in abundant love, peace and joy.

Do you want an intimate, close relationship with Jesus that causes you to desire with all your heart to please Him and be His bride, or do you want to desire it? If so, then you will enjoy reading this book.

My heart's prayer is that every woman who reads this book will find the love of Jesus Christ that will liberate her soul, bring about an intimate relationship with Him, which in turn will saturate her spirit and soul with "Unfaded Beauty".

SONG

<u>Let the Beauty of Jesus Be Seen In Me</u>
by **Alberta Orsborn**

Let the beauty of Jesus be seen in me,

All His wonderful passion and purity.

May His Spirit divine, all my nature refine.

Let the beauty of Jesus be seen in me.

When your burden is heavy and hard to bear

When your neighbors refuse all your load to share

When you're feeling so blue,

don't know just what to do.

Let the beauty of Jesus be seen in you.

When somebody has been so unkind to you,

Some word spoken that pierces you through and through.

Think how He was beguiled, spat upon and reviled,

Let the beauty of Jesus be seen in you.

From the dawn of the morning till close of day,

An example in deeds and in all you say,

Lay your gifts at His feet, ever strive to keep sweet.

Let the beauty of Jesus be seen in you.

Proverbs 31:30 "Favor is deceitful, and beauty is vain: but a woman that feareth the Lord, she shall be praised."

"And let the beauty of the Lord our God be upon us..." Psalm 90:17a

 ## *Chapter One* **Unfaded Beauty**

Have you, as a woman, ever just wanted to be beautiful? Do you strive to make yourself beautiful? I will be the first to admit, I have, almost obsessively. But have I ever felt like I attained it? No, absolutely not; it is quite fleeting.

What is your definition of beauty? What is the world's definition of beauty? Are they the same? Why do we as women, have such a strong desire to be considered beautiful? Why are we driven by this passion?

These are some of the questions I would like to talk about in this book and help women to think about.

Do you think that maybe we are driven by this passion because we are looking for affirmation, attention, love, and we feel in competition or compared with other women? There is a lot of competition between women, especially in the world. When I say world, I am talking about most women, because even we who are Christians have a tendency to feel the competition and comparison. It is a driving force in our lives and causes us to feel like we need to conform to other women's ideals so we will be accepted or even thought of as "better than others".

Why do we as woman feel such pressure to compete with other women? I believe most of it is because we are so inundated in our society with "beauty" and "comparison". We are saturated with it in all directions. This is too bad because it affects everything we do and causes us not to look to God for our affirmation and love, but to others, which always frustrates and never satisfies.

Maybe you would say, "I'm not frustrated". Honestly, let's think about how our society is so inundated with what they call beauty. Let's see, we have beauty salons, beauty schools, beauty departments in stores, beauty magazines, books about the "how to" of beauty, commercials about beauty, etc.

Some women actually are so obsessed with beauty, they abuse their bodies to attain this fleeting attribute. Examples: diets leading to anorexia and bulimia, facelifts, dermabrasions and surgeries. Some women, do all kinds of things that are uncomfortable or unhealthy (like high heels, putting up with the chemical stench of ammonias/dyes, nail care products and sun burning/tanning) not realizing that worldly beauty standards are very elusive even impossible to obtain. Why do we torture ourselves trying to be beautiful and stay that way? Do you ever ask yourself this question? We should. I am asking myself this question.

Do you realize how much money and time is spent chasing after the elusive dream of worldly beauty? New research on the New York Post website says that Groupon's study celebrated the official start of summer by asking 2000 American women the amount of money they spend on their appearance and uncovered some interesting trends.

The women surveyed who said they routinely spend money on their appearance spend an average of $3, 756 a year ($313 a month), which adds up to $225, 360 throughout their entire lifetime (ages 18-78). Would you say this is an astronomical amount? You could buy a very nice house with that much money, go on several trips around the world or even better, give to the poor. When I began to think about how much money I had spent, it made me realize I had wasted a lot of money.

Then we must ask the question…how does God feel about all of this? Is this insatiable desire to be beautiful what God intended for us as women? Does He really want us to be driven by this beast? Driven by lust to be something more than we are? Driven by what others think about us? Driven by this ferocious beast that never lets up…that never gives us a break…that never stops eating at us? I have to be honest that most of my life I have suffered from this torturous never-ending struggle without peace or satisfaction.

Why? Why do we as women feel like we can never be good enough, or look as good as other women? I have found that no matter how perfect I try to be I never feel quite good enough. Do you have these feelings?

Why do we, as women, allow ourselves to be so trapped, so driven, so imprisoned, so captive to this lust for worldly beauty? Why does it rule and reign in our lives? Why has it taken me all these years to see the deception of it...and the slavery?

Why have we as women, godly women, not searched out the Word of God to see what God has to say about this monster? Well, I believe it is time for us women to make war against this beast. I pray we can come to the place where we can say that we are "content (satisfied) in whatever state we are in."

Philippians 4:11

"Not that I speak in regard to need, for I have learned in whatever state I am, to be content:" ...we can know the *"peace which passes all understanding"* (*Philippians 4:7*) and we can know the *"fullness of the love of God"* (*Ephesians 3:19*) *which will cast out all fear.* (*1 John 4:18*)

Notes:

"Turn away mine eyes from beholding vanity; and quicken thou me in thy way." Psalm 119:37

Chapter Two
 # Vanity, Vanity

I have most definitely had a fear of man (or woman); in what they think of me. We need to have the "fear of God". In Proverbs 31:30, we see that…

> *"Favor* (charm) *is deceitful, and beauty is vain* (passing) *but a woman that feareth the Lord, she shall be praised"*.

Is this our motive for wanting to be beautiful (worldly beauty) to be praised? I must honestly say, "it is and has been a motive of mine". But we must ask ourselves? Does it bring peace, joy and love to our lives? It most definitely has not to mine. Whatever pleasure I have gotten from the praise of men and women has been fleeting… I always needed a new dress, a new pair of shoes, a new purse, etc., so I could receive some more of that kind of praise.

Why is it we crave other's attention? Why does the "fear of man" bring a snare to our soul?

This was brought to my attention when I married my husband. He seemed to love me just the way I was, every day. I've never been totally happy with myself no matter how I looked; I could always find fault with myself; guess being a perfectionist did not help. His acceptance and even admiration of me was there whether I was all dressed up with makeup and pretty clothes or I had just gotten out of bed with unkempt hair. It blew me away.

I began to realize I had been fed a lie all my life or had believed a lie. Where did this lie come from? Why did he think I was beautiful, even gorgeous, with not even a dab of makeup on or my hair fixed specially? I noticed that the happier I was, the more I genuinely smiled, the more he praised me. He seemed to truly believe I was beautiful.

Wow! What a revelation of God's love for me to realize I am accepted and loved just the way He made me!

Have you ever seen women all decked out with strikingly beautiful clothing, lots of precise makeup, nails manicured/pedicured, and lots of pretty jewelry but with a sour expression? What were your thoughts or impressions? Did you have thoughts of how beautiful they were? Were you impressed with all their outward statements of so-called beauty? Well, I know what I have thought. It did not matter to me what kind of fashion or beauty statement they were making; I did not think of them as beautiful.

1 Peter 1:14 "As obedient children, not fashioning yourselves according to the former lusts in your ignorance."

What are your thoughts when you see a woman, with no makeup, no fancy clothes, no well-coiffed hair, and no jewelry, but with a great big smile, a sweet gentle spirit, and kind compassionate eyes full of love? Oh, and also a beautiful shine on her face from Jesus' presence in her life. I admire women who have these true beauty qualities. Do you?

Why does this world, especially in America, make us feel like we have to conform to a certain mold? And why do we as Christian women fall into the same trap of conforming to this world's mold?

> *Romans 12:1-2 "I beseech you therefore, breth-ren, by the mercies of God, that ye present your bodies a living sacrifice, holy, acceptable unto God, which is your reasonable service. And be not conformed to this world: but be ye transformed by the renewing of your mind, that ye may prove what is that good, and acceptable, and perfect, will of God."*

Conformity always brings to my mind, being molded into a tight box, keeping us in a prison to the ways of man. It makes me feel like I can't really be myself or be free to be me. It always introduces itself as an enjoyable plaything, but it becomes a bondage that never let's go of its grip on our souls. At first it looks like a very inviting, exciting room to play around in but later we realize it is actually a dismal prison, that cuts off our souls from light and love. It binds us to "other's opinions" rather than the freedom that comes from God's acceptance and love.

Notes:

"Honor and majesty are before Him: strength and beauty are in His sanctuary." Psalm 96:6

 Chapter Three
Ageless Beauty Treatments

Let's think about what the word **"beauty"** means from the dictionary. It means…

1. Giving pleasure to the mind or senses.

2. Giving the greatest pleasure and stirring emotions.

3. A person's physical features are considered aesthetically pleasing.

4. A particularly graceful, ornamental, or excellent quality.

I like #4. It says, "A particularly graceful, ornamental, or excellent quality".

Does God love beauty? Yes! Then, we have the question does God want us to be beautiful? Yes!

Well, the only way to learn more about these questions is to go where God speaks to us, the Bible. When I started really delving into the study of true beauty in the Bible and other books, I began to realize that, hey, God IS into women being beautiful, BUT what are His thoughts about it? Maybe we should back up and see if we want to please God, ourselves or other people? Or are we triple minded? Ha-ha! Can we be triple minded and please God?

Well, that is what this book is about. Let's allow God's Holy Spirit, to check out our hearts. First of all, do we really know God, Jesus His Son, in our heart of hearts? Have we truly had a born again, repentant heart, that has been transformed by the light of Christ's love and glory? Let's look at how this can happen in our lives.

In Acts 2:37,38 says...

> *"Now when they heard this, they were pricked in their heart, and said unto Peter and to the*

rest of the apostles, Men and brethren, what shall we do?

(They were asking what they must do to be saved, born again or converted). Peter answered in verse 38:

"Then Peter said unto them, Repent, and be baptized every one of you in the name of Jesus Christ for the remission of sins, and ye shall receive the gift of the Holy Ghost."

Of course, if we have never had a truly born-again experience with Christ changing our hearts then we will have strong desires to fulfill the lust of our flesh man (woman). But I trust that each of the women who read this book have a heart that is born again and desire to please God (or will cry out to God for this heart) above all others, even yourself.

Then if we have truly let Christ into our hearts and minds, let us go on to learning how to be beautiful in His sight. Do we truly have a passionate desire to please and make our Lord and Savior happy with us? This is so deep because it entails so very many aspects of us as women.

I will try to share from my heart and experience over the years, how God has been so patient, kind, merciful and faithful to speak intimately to me concerning my relationship with Him as a daughter and also as the Bride of Christ. God's loving kindness, tender mercies and His extravagant love are one of the most precious, valuable life changing, face lifting, beauty treatments of all times. This kind of beauty is ageless, eternal, fades not away, is wrinkle free, lasting, attractive, desirable, pure, holy, and praised by God.

Why do men and women always try to invent or make up their own ways of being good and bringing pleasure to themselves? God's ways and thoughts are so much higher than ours.

Isaiah 55: 8
"For my thoughts are not your thoughts, neither are your ways my ways, saith the Lord."

We see in Psalms 24:3-6…

*"Who shall ascend into the hill of the Lord? Or who shall stand in His holy place? He that hath clean hands, and a pure heart; who hath not lifted up his soul unto **vanity**, nor sworn deceitfully. He shall receive the blessing from the Lord, and righteousness from the God of his salvation. This is the generation of them that seek Him, that seek thy **face**, O Jacob. Selah"*

As we read about the children of Israel, in the Old Testament and the New, mankind has, even from the beginning, been rebellious. We have thought, I say thought, because it is a myth, that we can be happy and have peace by going our own way in disobedience. If we truly want God to be our Father and be the beautiful bride of Christ, then we must submit to His love.

In Hebrews 12:5-13 it tells us about God's love that chastens us. In love He will chasten us and scourge us as a Father, showing His compassion and helping us find the lowliness of heart and meekness to accept that we can never please Him in our own selves. If we, as women, will let the Holy Spirit humble us and realize that we are very needy of Jesus Christ, He can shine the light of His love, grace, and mercy towards us in the form of healing for our souls. We will find that we become joyful, happy, content, peaceful, fulfilled and beautiful; all attributes shining from our inner being of Christ's amazing grace.

Studying the Bible about true unfading beauty which comes from God's majestic, radiating, unadulterated, pure, lovely, sweet, passionate, self-sacrificing, humble Spirit, is an eye opening, life changing, deeply soul renovating, beauty treatment.

You may ask, "is God interested in beauty treatments for women?" You better believe He is! And His beauty treatments are so much better, lasting, and truly have much more beautiful results than woman's earthly, vain, corruptible, deceitful, frustrating, costly, lustful, unsatisfying, selfish, striving and Holy Spirit quenching way, of trying to become beautiful!

Psalm 96:6
"Honor and majesty are before Him: strength and beauty are in His sanctuary."

What do you think, women? Are you finding true unfading beauty in God's sanctuary?

Notes:

"But we all, with open face beholding as in a glass the glory of the Lord, are changed into the same image from glory to glory, even as by the Spirit of the Lord." 2 Corinthians 3:18

 ## *Chapter Four*
Transforming Beauty

In this book I want to encourage us, as women, to find Christ's genuine beauty through a close intimate relationship with Him. This is not about rules or legalistic ways, it is about "knowing" Christ in a way that will transform us, as women, into the beautiful creatures He made us to be. God is not against us wanting to be adorned or putting on ornaments for beauty, He made us to desire to be beautiful and desire to be praised, but what kind of ornaments are we putting on?

It is not so much about DO NOTS but about finding a more excellent way. The enemy of our souls wants to sell us on something cheap, unfulfilling, never satisfying, and frustrating. BUT GOD wants us to walk in His ways, the more excellent way.

> *Proverbs 3: 5*
> *"Trust in the Lord with all thine heart and lean not unto thine own understanding."*

> *Psalms 93:5b,*
> *"Holiness adorns Your house, O Lord forever."*

Are we not the house (temple) of the Lord (Holy Spirit)? NKJV

1 Corinthians 3:16 reads,

> *"Do you not know that you are the temple of God and that the Spirit of God dwells in you?" (NKJV)*

May we be adorned with God's Holiness; that's true unfading beauty.

When I think about transformation, immediately my mind goes to a butterfly's metamorphosis. Why did God make a butterfly to be transformed from an egg to larva (caterpillar), to pupa then to an adult butterfly? It is a rapidly changing process that is phenomenal and shows God's almighty, intricate detail, and wisdom. Why do we as humans want to do things different than God planned them? Why are we foolish and vain? God has made all things according to His infinite wisdom.

> *Isaiah 55: 8-9*
> *"For as the heavens are higher than the earth, so are My ways higher than your ways, and My thoughts higher than your thoughts."*
> *(NKJV)*

Why does man, who has finite understanding, think His ways are better than God's infinite ways?

If we want to please God and be the Bride of Christ, (this is our goal, right?) should we not seek out God's way and wisdom so we will live a fruitful, fulfilling and praiseworthy life instead of a vain, wasteful, regretful, selfish, corruptible and unfulfilling life?

As the butterfly instinctively does what God created it to do, shouldn't we as His creatures, made in His image, be transformed into the beautiful creatures He intended for us to be, by submitting to His design and plan? I think so, as we happily find His purpose for us.

> Isaiah 43:7
> *"Everyone who is called by My name, Whom I have created for My glory; I have formed him, yes, I have made him." NKJV*

Wow, we were made to glorify God! Let's glorify and worship Him in body, mind and spirit by becoming the unfaded, beautiful, wholesome, shamefaced creatures He designed us to be!

Then we come to the question, we, as women, should ask. How does God want to transform us into His glory and image? How does He want to make us beautiful in His sight for His pleasure and purposes and our own benefit? Simple, by putting on the mind of Christ!

Ephesians 4:22-24
"That you put off, concerning your former conduct, the old man which grows corrupt according to the deceitful lusts, and be renewed in the spirit of your mind, and that you put on the new man which was created according to God, in righteousness and holiness." NKJV

What is so wonderful about this glorious transformation by Almighty God, maker of the Universe and Creation? It is the fact that, it is not just for God to show us off as His precious beautiful treasure, He also does it for our profit, that we may be a partaker of His divine nature and holiness.

Hebrews 12:10,11
"For they verily for a few days chasten us after their own pleasure; but He for our profit, that we might be partakers of His holiness. Now no chastening for the present seems to be joyous, but grievous: nevertheless, afterward it yields the peaceable fruit of righteousness unto them which are exercised thereby."

God does this so we can live in unspeakable joy, peace that passes understanding, and amazing love that has no end.

In 2 Chronicles 20:21,22 God instructed the children of Israel to *"worship the Lord in the **beauty of holiness"**.* As they did God fought the battles and enemy, causing the enemies to kill their own selves, thus giving Israel rest from their enemies, great joy and prosperity. (They kept the spoil of their enemies).

When we come to the place that we truly understand we find everything in Christ...our joy, happiness, peace, love, beauty, fulfillment, and completion, we experience the greatest joy and rest that we as women could ever know. The vain, fading ways of the world are a caricature of the real beauty of God's kingdom and glory. God's ways are the opposite of man's ways. Man looks on the outward appearance, but God looks on the heart.

In 1 Samuel 16:7 it says...

"But the Lord said unto Samuel, look not on his countenance, or on the height of his stature; because I have refused him: for the Lord sees not as man sees; for man looks on the outward appearance, but the Lord looks at the heart."

This world we live in tells us lies but if we look into God's Word, we see the opposite.

In 2 Corinthians 3:17, 18 we read…

"Now the Lord is that Spirit; and where the Spirit of the Lord is, there is liberty. But we all, with open face beholding as in a glass the glory of the Lord, are changed into the same image from glory to glory, even as by the Spirit of the Lord."

I have found in my own life and as I behold the glory of the Lord as in a (mirror) glass that the beauty of the Lord shines out of my countenance causing **His beauty** to be seen.

From the song at the beginning of this book there are words that say: "Let the beauty of Jesus be seen and me, all His wonderful passion and purity, oh now spirit divine, all my nature refine, till the beauty of Jesus be seen in me".

There is absolutely no comparison to the beautiful transformation that we find in the presence of the Lord compared to the so-called beauty of the world. As I have spent time worshiping and praising the Lord and studying His Word to find out how precious and what a treasure I am to Him, I have found a joy and love that this world knows nothing about.

This brings the true beauty of God on our countenance and reflects His glory. We find in Proverbs 31 that this kind of woman who fears God will be praised. It is a result of us, as women, finding our beauty in the Lord.

In Proverbs 31 verse 10, it begins asking the question, "Who can find a virtuous woman? It seems to be very important. Then it tells us her price is far above rubies.

Proverbs 31:30

*"Favor is deceitful, and (worldly) beauty is vain: but a woman that **feareth the Lord** she shall be praised."*

Earlier I mentioned that as women, for the most part, we try to be beautiful so we can be praised. Well, this makes it clear how we will be praised.

Do we want to be a vain person who regrets how we lived our lives? Or do we want to be a virtuous woman who is praised by her husband, children and by God?

Notes:

"Whose adorning let it not be that outward adorning…But let it be the hidden man of the heart…the ornament of a meek and quiet spirit, which is in the sight of God of great price."
1 Peter 3:3a,4

Chapter Five

 # Adorning Beauty

We read about Sarah in 1 Peter 3:3,4.

*"Whose adorning let it not be that outward adorning of plaiting the hair, and of wearing of gold, or of putting on of apparel; But let it be the **hidden** man of the heart, in that which is not corruptible, even the **ornament** of a meek and quiet spirit, which is in the sight of God of great price."*

I'm sure she was like every other woman who has been born, having a built-in desire (human nature) to be adorned with ornaments showing her beauty to the world. BUT she had the wisdom, (did not have the Bible like we do) to realize where her true beauty came from. I believe Sarah had learned to "know God intimately", to spend time with God in His beauty and grace so she could reflect it to the world. She came to the understanding that to shine with God's true beauty she needed to submit to God's grace, showing this by trusting in God and then being in "subjection" to her husband (verses 5-6).

*"For after this manner in the old time the holy women also, who trusted in God, **adorned** themselves, being and subjection unto their own husbands: Even as Sara obeyed Abraham, calling him Lord: whose daughters ye are, as long as ye do well, and are not afraid with any amazement."*

I believe Sarah realized she did not need to try to impress the world or her husband that she was beautiful, and she understood what Proverbs 31 tells us about the so-called beauty of the world; it is vain, and favor (charm) is deceitful.

1 Peter 3:5-6 says that Sarah "trusted" in God and was not afraid with any amazement.

I believe she had come to the realization that her husband and other people would let her down, but God was trustable. God would protect her and fight against her enemies. God loved and cared about her intimately and in every situation, every problem. She knew that her God had already won the victory and she was very precious and beautiful in His sight. We can also see this for ourselves in (Romans 8:37) and (Song of Solomon 2:14)

I believe Sarah had such a close intimate relationship with God that she put on "an ornament of a meek and quiet spirit, which in the sight of God is of great price" on herself. (Verse 4) She had a close loving, joy filled, peaceful, fulfilling life with God and out of that came the same with her husband. Sarah cared a whole lot more about being of great price in God's eyes than in any one else's, even her husband, Abraham. I believe that because she put God first, He gave her the desires of her heart. God can give us the desires of our hearts also. (Psalm 37:4) (Proverbs 4:7-9)

I'm sure that Sarah, like us as women, was tempted to focus on the outward appearance but as she came to experience a close intimate relationship with God, she wanted to please Him. She could see that the outward adornment and beauty were corruptible and the "meek and quiet spirit" were everlasting, not temporal. Her, "knowing" God intimately brought great joy, peace, and love to her inner being, which caused her to radiate Christ's grace and glory, the lasting true beauty.

How about you dear woman, are you tired of seeking vainly for man's (woman's) approval, praise, accolades and "desire towards you"?

We must surrender our hearts to the lover of Heaven and earth, who knows us intimately, in the deepest part of our beings and souls. Yet He loves us with a love that is beyond our comprehension and far beyond any love that a man can have towards us.

Our main pursuit, goal and seeking after, should be to "know Jesus Christ" in the deepest part of our beings.

> *Proverbs 4:7, 9*
> He will then *"crown us with His beauty"* that will *"last eternally and will not fade..."*
>
> *"She will place on your head an ornament of grace; a crown of glory she will deliver you,"*
>
> *1 Peter 1:4*
> *"To an inheritance incorruptible and undefiled, and that fades not away, reserved in heaven for you,"*

Aren't you tired of focusing on the world's mirror and seeing your temporal fading beauty taken over by wrinkles and age spots?

Even if you are not that old yet, do you want to live with regrets that you did not see God's ways which are so much higher than our ways?

Do you want to live in pride and vanity and wish you had listened to the more glorious way?

2 Corinthians 3:16-18

*"Nevertheless, when one turns to the Lord, the veil is taken away. Now the Lord is the Spirit; and where the Spirit of the Lord is, there is liberty. But we all, with unveiled face, beholding as in a **mirror** the **glory of the Lord**, are being transformed into the same image from glory to glory, just as by the spirit of the Lord." NKJV*

I love the lyrics to the song, "Turn Your Eyes Upon Jesus". They put it so beautifully: "Turn your eyes upon Jesus, look full in His wonderful face and the things of earth will grow strangely dim in the light of His glory and grace."

Is this the mirror we are looking into? That which is eternal? The only one where we will attain real lasting beauty that will never fade or end. The only one in which we will become the beautiful bride of Christ ruling and reigning with Him.

Let us begin to seek our Lord's face and be transformed by His glory and grace. Let us be enveloped in His transforming love, that will radiate from our innermost being, so we can reflect Christ's beauty to the world. This should cause others to become thirsty for what we have in Christ. Then others can find their way to Jesus, the light of the world, in this sin sick, dark world. We should be salt and light like Jesus asked us to be. (Matthew 5:13-16)

This is true unfading beauty! I pray that we as Christian women will no longer be deceived by the world. In Romans 12:1,2 Paul says,

"I beseech you therefore brethren, by the mercies of God, that you present your bodies a living sacrifice, holy, acceptable to God, which is your reasonable service. And do not be conformed to this world, but be transformed by the renewing of your mind, that you may prove what is that good and acceptable and perfect will of God."

Remember transformed means changed, "metamorphosis", like a butterfly. The beginnings of a butterfly are not beautiful, but the end results are, so we as we "wait on the Lord" stay in His presence, we will be transformed by the Spirit of the Lord from glory to glory."

Are our lives about ourselves? Or are we supposed to follow Christ's example of caring about souls and winning them to Jesus? Like this verse in 2 Corinthians 4:3,4 we see where our gospel can be hidden to them that are lost. It says,

*"But if our gospel **be hid**, it is hidden to them that are lost: In whom the god of this world hath blinded the minds of them which believe not, lest the light of the glorious gospel of Christ, who is the image of God, should shine unto them".*

Do we soak ourselves in Jesus' presence and love so our faces will shine with the light of the glorious gospel? I love the next scriptures also.

2 Corinthians 4:6,7
"For God, who commanded the light to shine out of darkness, hath shined in our hearts, to

*give the light of the knowledge of the glory of God in the **face** of Jesus Christ. But we have this **treasure** in earthen vessels, that the excellency of the power may be of God, and not of us."*

Do we have such an intimate relationship with Christ that we radiate to the world our treasure, which is coming from our inner most being? If so, then the world will see the excellency of God in our lives. Or do we just reflect the world and its darkness back to them? Again, is our gospel hidden from those who are lost? I don't know about you, but I want this treasure I have in my earthen vessel to shine forth to those who need it, so they can know the light of the knowledge of the glory of God in the face of Jesus Christ. There is no greater joy, peace or love than this. There is nothing in this world as fulfilling as this treasure we have in the face of Jesus Christ.

My encouragement to us, as women, is to seek the Lord and His face. His Word is so precious to daily soak our souls in. What a beauty treatment!

Psalm 105:2-4

"Sing unto Him, sing psalms unto Him; talk ye of all His wondrous works. Glory ye in His holy name: let the heart of them rejoice that seek the Lord. Seek the Lord, and His strength: **seek His face** *evermore."*

Psalm 147:1

"Praise the Lord! For it is good to sing praises to our God; For it is pleasant, and **praise is beautiful.***" (NKJV)*

Psalm 149:4

"For the Lord takes pleasure in His people; He will **beautify the humble** *with salvation." (NKJV)*

Psalm 90:17

"And let the **beauty** *of the Lord our God be upon us and establish the work of our hands for us; yes, establish the work of our hands." (NKJV)*

1 Chronicles 16:9-11,
"Sing to Him, sing psalms to Him, talk of all His wondrous works! Glory in His holy name; let the hearts of those rejoice who **seek the Lord***! (NKJV)*

I encourage all women to **seek the Lord** with all your heart!

Notes:

"Seek the Lord and His strength, seek His face continually."
1 Chronicles 16:11

 ## Chapter Six
Bridal Tips

How bad do you want to be the "bride of Christ"? Have you developed a close intimate relationship with Jesus?

Most little girls dream of their wedding day and the handsome man they will marry someday but does our heart, as a woman, yearn for Christ to be our groom and come for us? We should examine our own hearts to see where they are at. Do we love the world and the things in the world? God's Word tells us that "if we love the world and the things in the world, the love of the Father is not in us".

1 John 2:15-17
"Do not love the world or the things in the world. If anyone loves the world, the love of the

Father is not in him. For all that is in the world
– the lust of the flesh, the lust of the eyes, and
the pride of life – is not of the Father but is of
the world. And the world is passing away, and
the lust of it; but he who does the will of God
abides forever." NKJV

Do you, as the bride of Christ, want to do the will of God in your life in every area? Or are you being deceived by loving the world and the things in the world?

Do we realize that Christ is not coming back for those "who love the world" and the "things in the world?" He is coming for a bride "who hath made herself ready".

Revelation 19:7,8
"Let us be glad and rejoice and give honor to
Him: for the marriage of the Lamb is come, and
*his wife hath made **herself** ready. And to her*
was granted that she should be arrayed in fine
linen, clean and white: for the fine linen is the
righteousness of the saints."

He is coming for those who "look for Him". He is coming for a "bride without spot or wrinkle or any such thing".

> *Ephesians 5:26, 27*
> *"That He might sanctify and cleanse it with the washing of water by the word, that He might present it to Himself a glorious church, not having spot, or wrinkle, or any such thing; but that it should be holy and without blemish."*

So, shouldn't we strive to "please the Lord" in all things allowing the Holy Spirit to transform us into His glorious bride? To be the bride of Jesus Christ for all eternity, reigning with Him, worshipping Him, basking in His presence, is by far better than any earthly temporary fleeting things we can attain in this life. Do you as a woman desire to please the Lord in every area of your life? When a woman is in love with a man, doesn't she desire to please him?

What is our life on this earth? The Bible says it is a vapor…like steam.

James 4:14
"Whereas ye know not what shall be on the morrow. For what is your life? It is even a vapor, that appears for a little time, and then vanishes away."

Unless we "know Jesus" in a real intimate way, this life is vain and fruitless. Do we want to come to the end of our lives and realize that we sought after the things of this world instead of seeking to know Jesus?

How can we "find the Lord" and "love Him with all of our heart? I believe this comes from seeking God's face every day...all day, in prayer, worship and reading His word.

Psalm 105:4
"Seek the Lord, and His strength: seek His face evermore."

1 Chronicles 16:11
"Seek the Lord and His strength, seek His face continually."

Psalm 16:11

"You will show me the path of life; In Your presence is fullness of joy; At Your right hand are pleasures forevermore." NKJV

Isaiah 61:10

"I will greatly rejoice in the Lord, my soul shall be joyful in my God; for He has clothed me with the garments of salvation, He has covered me with the robe of righteousness, as a bridegroom decks himself with ornaments, and as a bride adorns herself with her jewels." NKJV

Revelation 21:2

"Then I, John, saw the holy city, New Jerusalem, coming down out of heaven from God, prepared as a bride adorned for her husband." NKJV

Finding Him is the only way we can love others as we love ourselves, if we "Know" Christ's love for us. You can't give someone else something you don't have yourself.

This is my greatest desire, to know Christ, and to make Him known to others. But I can only let His light shine through me. I can't do it for others. We each must have a strong desire, stronger than all other desires, to know Christ in *"...the power of His resurrection, the fellowship of His sufferings, being made conformable to His death". (Philippians 3:10).*

We see the parable about the wise and foolish virgins (see Matthew 25:1-13). Both groups were looking for their groom to come back to take them with Him BUT the foolish virgins expected Him sooner and did not prepare themselves with enough oil. The wise virgins had more than enough oil to wait for the groom to come. They were NOT "just getting by", like the foolish virgins, they were inundated and saturated with the "oil of the Holy Spirit", "the oil of joy", the *"And wine that makes glad the heart of man, oil that makes man's face shine". (Psalm 104:15)*

So, let me ask, do you seek Him? Do you love Jesus and hunger after His righteousness? I think that our lives are the fruit of that question.

Matthew 5:6

"Blessed are those who hunger and thirst for righteousness, for they shall be filled."

Notes:

"Abide in Me, and I in you. As the branch cannot bear fruit of itself, unless it abides in the vine, neither can you, unless you abide in Me." John 15:4 NKJV

 ## *Chapter Seven*
Beauty Rest

How do we know if we love Jesus? We see in John 14:15 it says,

"If you love Me keep My commandments". NKJV

Verse 21 says,

"He who has My commandments, and keeps them, it is he who loves Me. And he who loves Me will be loved of My Father, and I will love him, and will manifest Myself to him". (See also John 15:10.)

If you're like me and have a desire for righteousness, you have tried to do this on your own; tried to keep God's Commandments BUT we cannot do this in ourselves.

Romans 10:2-4

"For I bear them witness that they have a zeal for God, but not according to knowledge. For they, being ignorant of God's righteousness, and seeking to establish their own righteousness, have not submitted to the righteousness of God. For Christ is the end of the law for righteousness to everyone who believes."

These scriptures say Israel went about to establish their own righteousness but did NOT SUBMIT themselves unto the righteousness of God. We should examine ourselves to see if we do the same thing. The ONLY way we can submit to Gods righteousness is when we learn to "abide in Christ". God's righteousness only comes from a relationship, I would dare to say, a close intimate relationship with Jesus.

In John 15:4 we see this truth,

"Abide in Me, and I in you. As the branch cannot bear fruit of itself, unless it abides in the

vine; neither can you, unless you abide in Me."
NKJV

The whole chapter is about "abiding in Christ". Verse 6 says,

"If a man abides not in Me, he is cast forth as a branch, and is withered; and men cast them into the fire, and they are burned."

We see this passage emphasizes our desperate need to *"abide in Christ"* and *"let His Word abide in us"*.

As we intimately worship Jesus and abide in His presence through His Word, we will see the fruit of obedience grow in us through His grace and mercy. We will then bear the fruit of the Spirit.

Galatians 5:5
"For we through the Spirit wait for the hope of righteousness by faith".

Galatians 5 is about *"walking in the Spirit"* *"not in the flesh"*. (Read Galatians 5:16-26.)

How can we truly "walk in the Spirit"?

I find in my own life that as I...

"Enter into His gates with thanksgiving and into His courts with praise" (Psalm 100:4), and as I *"bless the Lord at all times"*, and *"praise the Lord continually"*(Psalm 34:1), that's when I began to walk in the Spirit, along with *"pray without ceasing"* (1 Thessalonians 5:17), *"be careful* (anxious) *for nothing but in everything by prayer and supplication"* (Philippians 4:6-7) that abiding in Christ becomes a way of life which produces peace and rest in my everyday life.

I believe that God has given me an acronym for the word "Rest". It is:

R- Rejoicing

E - Every

S- Single

T- Time

In Matthew 11:28-30 it shows us Jesus' heart towards us...

"Come unto Me, all ye that labor and are heavy laden, and I will give you rest. Take My yoke upon you and learn of Me; for I am meek and lowly in heart: and ye shall find rest unto your souls. For My yoke is easy, and My burden is light."

Do you, my sister and friend, want to find this true peace and rest? True unfading beauty rest comes only by abiding in Christ Jesus.

Notes:

"In like manner also, that women adorn themselves in modest apparel, with shamefacedness and sobriety..." 1 Timothy 2:9a

 ## *Chapter Eight* **Adornment**

Considering all the things that have been said so far, I would like to study with you the verses in 1 Timothy 2:8,9 that God, through Paul, speaks to men in verse 8 and women in verse 9.

> *1 Timothy 2:8- 9*
> *"I will therefore that men pray everywhere, lifting up holy hands, without wrath and doubting.* **In like** *manner also, that women adorn themselves in modest apparel, with shamefacedness and sobriety; not with broided (braided with riches) hair, or gold, or pearls, or costly array; But which become* **women professing godliness** *with good works."*

In verse 8 is the instruction (command) for men to pray **everywhere**, lifting up holy hands, without wrath and doubting.

That is pretty clear in its meaning but the next verse 9 tells women in "like manner", to adorn themselves in modest apparel, with shamefacedness and sobriety, but which becometh women professing godliness with good works. Doesn't it seem that the words "like manner" would mean that it is a similar instruction as the men praying lifting holy hands?

So, for a woman to adorn herself in "modest apparel", as women professing godliness, is a similar instruction. In this day and age, it seems like people do not study God's Word to see His instruction for us so we can please Him. There is definitely a trend for immodest apparel in the world and in the church. Ladies, we represent the church **everywhere** we go! This is grievous that there is so much immodesty and even lewdness. Is this pleasing to God? It seems that if women are dressed so immodestly and maybe even lewd, that God may be saying in this passage that men will be distracted (or even worse) from their prayer and lifting up of holy hands!

Do we as women want to be guilty before God of causing a distraction for men that keeps them from "lifting up Holy hands" like this passage instructs them to do? Why would these scriptures be connected together "as in like manner" if this was not so? Both instructions are just as important, one to men and the other to women.

We need to study what the word **"modest"** means in this passage. In the Greek Strong's concordance, it uses the word **"kosmios"** (G2885) for modest meaning well arranged, seemly, modest.

Thayers Greek Lexicon uses the word **"aidos"** (G127) meaning "a sense of shame or honor, modesty, bashfulness, reverence, regard for others, and through the idea of downcast eyes."

Let me ask you, as a woman professing godliness, do you feel your apparel is pleasing to God as decent, modest, bashful, honorable, shamefaced?

Or is it indecent, immodest, lewd or not portraying a sense of shame (shamefacedness), or is it disrespecting yourself or others?

I would encourage you as a woman, if you love Jesus and want to please Him above all else that you search the scriptures and your motives about how you adorn yourself with apparel.

Galatians 5:19,20

*"Now the works of the flesh are evident, which are: adultery, fornication, uncleanness, **lewdness**, idolatry, sorcery, hatred, contentions, jealousies, outbursts of wrath, selfish ambitions, dissensions, heresies, envy, murders, drunkenness, rivalries, and the like; of which I tell you beforehand, just as I also told you in time past, that those who practice such things will not inherit the kingdom of God."*

The word **"lewd"** which is used in this passage, concerning the works of the flesh, in Greek is **"nabluth"** (5039) and means: Immodesty, shamelessness.

"nechosheth" (5179) means: lust and harlotry.

We, as women, are inundated very much with propaganda about how to be beautiful, sensual, seductive, desirable, etc. Why are we conforming to the world?

Romans 12:1,2 addresses this very well.

> *"I beseech you therefore, brethren, by the mercies of God, that you present your **bodies** a living sacrifice, holy, acceptable to God, which is your **reasonable** service. And do not be conformed to this world, but be transformed by the renewing of your mind, that you may prove what is that good and acceptable and perfect will of God." NKJV*

Conform means to be put in a box, be restricted by a certain idea, to be squeezed into something restrictive.

Transform means to become something brand new, to be free, unrestricted.

Why would we as women want to be conformed to the ideas, restrictions, "opinion of others morality"? Aren't we to be adorned in Jesus's likeness?

This is what the world does to us, puts us in a mold, a trap, to be "like" the world.

God's Word transforms us to be "like" Him and His Word so we can find freedom to be the "woman He created us to be." There is joy, peace, freedom, and a sense of respect for ourselves and others when we please God in our apparel. We feel great joy that we are making our groom (Jesus Christ) happy.

What a freedom and peace that comes knowing we are being made in His image (spirit, soul and body)

So then, we should ask ourselves, how in love with Jesus are we as women and does the way we adorn ourselves produce a life that pleases Him?

Romans 12:2 uses the word **"reasonable"** in Greek it's Strongs #G3050 Logikos meaning 1. **Ra-**

tional 2. **sensible**. this is the word English derives its word "Logic" from, so dressing in a fashion as to not call attention to self and distract men from prayer, worship and the Word is the most logical, sensible, reasonable, very least we should be doing! Can I get an Amen!

This book is not about legalistic rules or regulations. It is about the question, "How much do you love Jesus and how much do you want to please Him in your life?"

John 14:15
"If You love me, keep My commandments."
NKJV

Nothing matters, in this life we are living, if this question is not settled in our hearts. There is a scripture that says, *"it is impossible to please God without faith" (Hebrews 11:6)* but it also says in another scripture says, *"Faith without works is dead"*. *(James 2:20b)* So if we don't have good works to support our faith, what do we have?

As mature Christian women or those who are working on their maturity, we should above all things, work on "knowing Jesus" intimately. Just like a woman who is in love with a man she plans to marry, will work on doing everything she can to please him, because she is "in love" with him. Is this your heart my sister, my friend?

If this is your heart, then let's go a little further in how we can please the Lord in our lives.

I believe that God, in His Word, has gender specific instructions for us as women. Do you think that God planned for us as women to study the Word of God specifically addressed to men?

Or do you think that we as women should want to please the Lord and make Him happy by studying the Word of God daily to see His instructions for us, as women, His beloved?

Let us talk about some of the specific instructions that God gives us, as women, in His Word.

Let's look at 1 Timothy 2:9 again.

> *"In like manner also, that women **adorn** them-selves in modest apparel, with **shamefaced-ness** and sobriety; not with broided* (braided with riches) *hair, or gold, or pearls, or costly array; But which become a woman professing **godliness** with good works."*

It seems, like I said before, that since this is a di-rect instruction, specifically to us women, we should, if we love Jesus and desire to please Him with all our heart, learn what this scripture means, then do it. The next thing is to take to heart and study what this scripture actually means.

What does the word "**adorn**" mean?

In the dictionary, we see that the word adorn means "to decorate or add beauty to, as orna-ments: to make more pleasing, attractive, impres-sive, etc.; enhance. In the Strong's concordance we see that the word "adorn" in Greek is "**kosmeo**" (this is where English gets its word "**cosmetics**) meaning "to put in proper order, i.e., decorate (literally or figuratively); specially to snuff (a wick): – adorn, garnish, trim. (G 2885). We see this word used in 1 Timothy 2:9, Titus 2:10, 1 Peter 3:5, Revelation 21:2.

As we study these scriptures specifically addressed to women and to us as the bride of Christ, I pray that God gives each one of us an understanding heart, God's heart for us women.

In 1 Timothy 2:9, we see that it uses the word *"modest"* regarding women *"adorning themselves in modest apparel"*.

Now we need to find out what the word *"modest"* means. In the Merriam-Webster dictionary (merriamwebster.com) there are four definitions for the word.

1. a. Placing a moderate estimate on one's abilities or worth. b. Neither **bold** nor **self-assertive**: tending toward diffidence.

2. Arising from or of a modest nature.

3. Observing the proprieties of dress and behavior: decent

The synonyms I found in my search for the definition of "modest" are these:

1. shy, 2. bashful, 3. diffident, 4. coy 5. chaste, 6. pure, 7. decent

1. **Shy** implies a timid reserve and a shrinking from familiarity or contact with others.

2. **Bashful** implies a frightened or hesitant shyness characteristic of childhood and adolescence.

3. **Diffident** stresses a distrust of one's own ability or opinion that causes hesitation in acting or speaking.

4. **Coy,** meaning not inclined to be forward.

5. **Chaste** primarily implies a refraining from acts or even thoughts or desires that are not virginal or not sanctioned by marriage vows.

6. **Pure** differs from chaste in implying innocence and absence of temptation rather than control of one's impulses and actions.

7. **Decent** meaning "free from all taint of what is lewd or salacious.

Modest and decent apply especially to deportment (manner) and dress as **outward signs of inward chastity or purity.**

We see here that modest and decent apply to how we act and dress showing our outward signs of our inward chastity or purity. In the Merriam-Webster dictionary we see the definition of "chastity" and "purity" being:

1. **Chastity** means: 1a. Abstention from unlawful sexual intercourse. b. Abstention from all sexual intercourse b. Purity in conduct and intention. d. Restraint, simplicity and design or expression. 2. Personal integrity.
2. **Purity** means: 1. The quality or state of being morally pure. 2. Goodness, righteousness, virtue, decency, propriety, seemliness. 3. Taintless 4. Uncontaminated 5. Uncorrupted 6. Undefiled 7. Unpolluted 8. Free from any trace of the course or indecent. 9. Unspotted 10. Unstained 11. Unblemished 12. Unsullied. 13. Inoffensive.

In this Scripture in 1 Timothy 2:9, Paul speaking "inspired by the Holy Spirit", tells us, as women that we can be pleasing to God by asking Him to cleanse us from anything immodest in our apparel or conduct. We see that the words "modest", "purity", "decent", "chaste", "bashful", "shy", "discreet" are very similar in their meanings.

Do we want to be like Proverbs 11:22 where it says....

> *"As a jewel of gold in a swine's snout, so is a fair woman which is without discretion."*?

Let's go on to study the rest of this passage from 1 Timothy 2:9-11 and find out what it really means.

We see after the words "modest apparel" that it says we should adorn ourselves with "shamefacedness". We do not hear the word "shamefacedness" being used in our modern society. Do you think this could be because it is a very foreign concept to us, especially as American women?

Let's look up the meaning for the word "**shame-facedness**". In the Merriam-Webster dictionary it says

1. **Showing modesty: bashful, shy**.

2. **Showing shame: ashamed**.

Here are other definitions/synonyms of "shame-facedness": 1. Shy or socially timid, not liking to be noticed. 2. Withdrawn 3. Meek 4. Demure 5. Unassertive 6. Reserved 7. Self-conscious.

I also decided it would be good to look up the antonyms/opposites of "shamefacedness". Some of them are: 1. Sassy 2. Attention seeker 3. Proud 4. Arrogant 5. Brazen 6. Brash 7. Loud 8. Boastful 9. Cheeky 10. Impudent.

Do these descriptions and definitions sound like what women's apparel and conduct are portraying today? Again, I encourage us, as women, to ask ourselves, according to this passage in 1 Timothy 2:8-11 do we truly love Jesus and want to please Him in our lives?

To be honest, I believe we are seeing the exact opposite, even in most so-called Christian women. We may tend to want to justify our actions because we think we live in a different culture than when this passage was written. If we truly have an honest and good heart, then we will love the instruction that He gave us in His Word and ask God to help us do that which is pleasing to Him.

There is a Scripture that says Jesus Christ is the same yesterday today and forever. His Word never changes, even if men change in their customs and culture.

Hebrews 13:8
"Jesus Christ is the same yesterday, today, and forever."

Malachi 3:6a
"For I am the Lord, I do not change;"

If we think that because the culture has changed it is okay to be immodest or bold, brazen, brash and the center of attention, we better cry out to

God to show us His ways of holiness and righteousness.

1 Thessalonians 4:7

"For God did not call us to uncleanness, but in holiness." NKJV

The next word in this passage I would like to study is the word "**sobriety**". It is not used very much in our vocabulary in today's modern world. It seems to be a word "of the past". When I looked up this word in the Merriam-Webster dictionary it says:

1. The quality or state of being sober.

2. The quality of being serious.

Here are the synonyms for it: 1. Ernest 2. Graveness 3. Gravity 4. Intentness 5. Serious mindedness 6. Seriousness 7. Soberness 8. solemnness 9. Staidness.

The antonyms/opposites are: 1. flightiness 2. Flippancy 3. Frivolous 4. Lightheartedness 5. Lightness 6. Playful 7. Unseriousness.

"**Shamefacedness**" and "**sobriety**" are ways that we as women should adorn ourselves. Only through the help of the Holy Spirit, can we judge our self whether our apparel or actions are portraying these godly characteristics or are they revealing the opposite?

The main motive of our heart, as women professing godliness, should be to reflect God's glory. Let me ask this question to all women, do you feel that your dress and actions show that you are an attention getter, frivolous, flippant, unserious, bold, brazen, indecent, forward, impure, lewd, and ungodly? Or any one of these?

Do you feel that you do not portray yourself, as a woman professing godliness, but you do look and act like the world? You can change! Be bold for God.

2 Corinthians 6:17
"Therefore, come out from among them and be separate says the Lord. Do not touch what is unclean, and I will receive you." "I will be a

Father to you, and you shall be My sons and daughters, says the Lord Almighty."

I will address more concerning looking like the world later.

Moving on in 1 Timothy 2:9 it says, …

"Not with braided hair, or gold, or pearls, or costly array" …

I think we can see here that this part of the passage is referring to decking ourselves out with our riches in our hair or clothing. It appears that this part of the passage is not talking about fixing our hair but what our motives are. Is to call attention to self or, in portraying ourselves better than others?

In verse 10, it says,

"But which becomes women professing godliness with good works."

After looking up the word **"becoming"** in the Merriam-Webster dictionary it says it means

1. Suitable, fitting, especially: attractively suitable//becoming modesty, causing someone to look attractive: having a flattering or attractive effect.

Synonyms for **"becoming"** are: 1. Applicable 2. Appropriate. 3. Befitting 4. Proper 5. Suitable.

I have heard this before in some teaching concerning our adorning with apparel. It was said that our clothing should attract people to our face NOT to our body. This may be what this passage is mainly speaking about. Let me ask the question to women, "does your apparel or dress attract others to your face or to your body"?

Our faces and eyes are what reflect God's glory. People can see our spirit and soul through our eyes and faces. If we are full of joy peace and love, it will be shown on our faces and in our eyes. Why would we as godly women want others, especially men, to be attracted to or look at our bodies? Have you ever asked yourself that question?

If we look over the history of the world since the beginning of creation, we see that before Adam and Eve sinned in the garden, they were naked and unashamed, the way God made them. But when sin was allowed to conceive and brought forth death, they went and hid themselves from God using fig leaves to cover their nakedness. They did not even realize they were naked until they had sinned. After God asked Adam where he was at, God made them animal skins to cover their nakedness.

Have you ever thought about the difference between fig leaves and animal skins? (Genesis 3:7, Genesis 3:21)

Which one of these covers a person's nakedness more?

And then if I may be bold enough to say or ask the question, "Do you feel that your clothing or apparel is more like fig leaves or more like animal skins?"

Why did God want mankind to be covered so thoroughly? Have you ever asked this question?

Apparently, God wanted mankind to be covered modestly so that our nakedness would not be shown to others.

As I have researched in the Bible and history, it has come to my attention that normal people wore modest and decent clothing; with the exception of harlots, people who were demonically possessed or of heathen nations.

If you have ever seen pictures or videos of people from the past up until the early 1900s, they for the most part, are clothed decently and modestly. In documentary videos of the pioneers who crossed America, we see the women in clothing dressed from neck to toe. We also see the men dressed from neck to toe. They had long sleeve shirts on. They dressed this way even in very extreme hot weather. From what I have read, women in the past, were scandalized if even their ankle showed, especially in the presence of men. I am not suggesting you need to dress from head to toe but, we need to ask ourselves the question why they had, for almost 6000 years, a conscience about themselves to cover their nakedness?

Why did this change in the early 1900s? In the early 1900s, women began to wear knee length skirts. Why did it suddenly seem okay to "bare the ankle or even leg" when in previous years it was a scandal to dress that way?

We can see, obviously, in Isaiah 47:1-3 that showing the thigh or taking off the skirts is shameful!

> *"Take the millstones, and grind meal: uncover the locks, make bare the leg, uncover the thigh, pass over the rivers. Thy nakedness shall be uncovered, yea thy shame shall be seen I will take vengeance, and I will not meet thee as a man."*

It shows in this passage that it is a **judgment** from God and a **humiliation.** Why do we not see this from God's perspective in this nation? Why do people look at partial/nakedness as a good thing?

The dictionary says **"thigh"** means 1. In human anatomy, the thigh is the area between the hip (pelvis) and the knee.

The scripture that comes to mind regarding why people have compromised and allowed indecent, immodest, indiscreet, unchaste, lewd dress to inundate, even so-called Christians is 2 Timothy 3:1-5. We see that Paul wrote this:

"This know also, that in the last days perilous times shall come. For men (women) shall be lovers of their own selves, covetous, boasters, proud, blasphemers, disobedient to parents, unthankful, unholy, without natural affection, truce breakers, false accusers, incontinent, fierce, despisers of those that are good, traitors, heady, high-minded, lovers of pleasures more than lovers of God; Having a form of godliness but denying the power thereof: from such turn away."

We see here that in the last days perilous times shall come. The word perilous reminds me of being on the side of a mountain barely clinging to a rock, with the wind blowing. It is very danger-ous. The second verse tells us that people will be lovers of their own selves. If we truly are honest before God and ourselves, would we think that our manner of dress and actions is loving God and other people or loving our own selves?

Would you say that young women and older women's dress, today, portrays a heady, high-minded attitude or a demure, modest, shame-faced attitude?

We see in verse four that people will be heady and high-minded, lovers of pleasures more than lovers of God. In verse five we see that it says people will have a form of godliness but denying the power thereof: from such turn away. This is a grief to my heart as well as other Christians when we see a form of godliness, but there is no **power,** in so-called Christians lives, to desire to live a ho-ly, righteous, pure life and dress modestly.

Let's go down into verse 12 and 13 to see some more about how perilous it will be in the last days. Verse 12 says,

"Yes, and all that will live godly in Christ Jesus shall suffer persecution."

It makes me wonder if we are living godly lives why we are not suffering persecution?

If we are dressing and acting just like the world, will we suffer persecution?

In verse 13 it says,

*"But evil men and **seducers** shall wax worse and worse, deceiving, and being deceived."*

It seems to me that we do understand what evil men are, but do we understand what seducers are? Let me look it up in the dictionary and see what it has to say about the word.

Seduce: 1. To persuade to disobedience or disloyalty 2. To lead astray usually by persuasion or false promises 3. To carry out the physical seduction of and ties to sexual intercourse. 4. Attract.

Seducer means: 1. one that tries to get a person to give in to a desire. (By the way they dress and adorn themselves)

The synonyms for seduce are: 1. Allure 2. Bait 3. Beguile 4. Betray 5. Decoy 6. Entice 7. Lead on 8. Lure 9. Solicit 10. Tempt 11. Inveigle

1. **Lure** implies a drawing into danger, evil, or difficulty through attracting and deceiving.
2. **Entice** suggests drawing by artful or adroit means. (The way you act).
3. **Inveigle** implies enticing by cajoling or flattering. (The way you talk).
4. **Decoy** implies a luring into entrapment by artifice. (The way you adorn yourself).
5. **Tempt** implies the presenting of an attraction so strong that it overcomes the restraints of conscience or better judgment.
6. **Seduce** implies a leading astray by persuasion or false promises.

Most women know that men **are** seduced by the way a woman dresses or acts. I have spoken with my husband concerning how men can be seduced (or tempted to lust) by a woman's dress or actions. He has been totally honest with me concerning men's struggles in this area.

The Bible says in 1 Corinthians 10:13,

> *"No temptation has overtaken you except such as is **common to man**; but God is faithful, who will not allow you to be tempted beyond what you are able, but with the temptation will also make the way of escape, that you may be able to bear it."*

So, I can only deduct that since my husband has shared with me the temptations and thoughts that the enemy brings to him by women's immodest dress and their actions, that it is a great struggle for a Christian man in the world we live in today.

It is a shame that men cannot go to church (most of the time) and enjoy worshipping God without seeing women in immodest or even lewd apparel.

Why should we, as Christian women or women professing godliness, want to put a stumbling block or occasion to stumble and the temptation to be solicited or seduced in front of a Christian brother?

Is this a love for God or our fellow man? No, it's not.

If we are honest in our hearts before God, we will have to say that what "most Christian women" wear today does put a stumbling block and occasion for temptation before men.

In Romans 14: 7-13 we see scriptures that tell us not to put a stumbling block in our brother's way.

> *"For none of us lives to himself, and no man dies to himself. For whether we live, we live unto the Lord; and whether we die, we die unto the Lord: whether we live therefore, or die, we are the Lord's. "So, then every one of us shall give account of himself to God. Let us not therefore judge one another anymore: but judge this rather, that no man put a stumbling block or an* **occasion to fall in his brother's way."**

If clothing or our actions are causing a man to struggle with lust and we truly love the Lord wanting to please Him, then we should be willing to change these things out of love for God and our fellow man.

We see how serious this is in Matthew 5:28,29 where Jesus spoke about a man lusting after a woman. It says:

> *"But I say to you, that, whoever looks at a woman to lust for her has already committed adultery with her in his heart. If your right eye causes you to sin, pluck it out, and cast it from you: for it is more profitable for you that one of your members perish, than for your whole body to be cast into hell." NKJV*

Jesus was letting us know how serious it is for a woman to cause a man to lust after her and a man to give into the temptation to lust. It says in verse 28 that if a man looks at a woman to lust after her he has committed adultery with **her** in his heart. It seems that women want to blame men for lusting after them, but the truth is if a woman is dressing in a manner that is provoking or seducing (tempting) the man, it is saying that she is just as guilty as he is.

Seriously, do we as women professing godliness, want men to look at us and lust after us, knowing that it is as serious as them having to pluck out their eye, so they do not go to hell?

This is very serious as Jesus appealed to men and women to do whatever it takes to not cause a temptation in this area. It is as serious as going to hell or not. Know these scripture passages were written 2000 years before the influx of lewd and immodest apparel. Don't be deceived. True love will go out of its way to deny itself for our beloved bridegroom and for others.

Notes:

"But put ye on the Lord Jesus Christ, and make not provision for the flesh, to fulfill the lust thereof." Romans 13:14

 Chapter Nine
Sacrificial Beauty

Let us look at this Scripture again, Romans 12:1-2 tells us:

> *"I beseech you therefore, brethren, by the mercies of God, that you present your **bodies** a living sacrifice, **holy**, acceptable to God, which is your reasonable service. And **do not** be conformed to this world: but be **transformed** by the renewing of your mind, that you may prove what is that good, and acceptable, and perfect, will of God." NKJV*

Should we break this Scripture down into words?

It says that Paul was beseeching, meaning **begging** Christians to present our bodies a living sacrifice. Meaning that our lives should be a sacrifice in all areas: dress, speech and actions. Giving in to our lusts is the **exact opposite** of "presenting our bodies a living sacrifice". This Scripture does not say our spirits or souls should be a living sacrifice, it says our **"bodies"**. This tells me that the things that we do in our bodies should be sacrificial or showing love to God and our fellow man.

We also see we should present our bodies to God **"holy"**. We, as women professing godliness, should ask ourselves if our clothing or conduct represents **"holiness"** or **"purity"**. Presenting our bodies as "holy" will then be acceptable to God and we will be in the perfect will of God.

Paul goes on to say that this is just our **"reasonable** service to God". In other words, it seems this passage is saying that it is just reasonable, actually not even going out of our way if we obey this. God is just **"expecting** us to live our lives as a living sacrifice". I can't stress enough that "sacrifice" is the **exact opposite** of giving in to our lusts. It is dying to our own self and desires.

Let's look at some more scripture concerning giving in to our lusts:

Romans 6:12

"Let not sin therefore reign in your mortal **body**, that you should obey it in the **lusts** thereof."

Romans 13:14

"But put on the Lord Jesus Christ, and make **no** provision for the flesh, to fulfill its **lusts**." *NKJV*

Galatians 5:16

"I say then: Walk in the Spirit, and you shall **not** fulfill the **lust of the flesh**."

Ephesians 2:3

"Among whom also we all had our conversation in times past in the **lusts** of our flesh, fulfilling the desires of the flesh and of the mind; and were by nature the children of wrath, even as others." *NKJV*

Titus 2:11-14

"For the **grace** of God that bringeth salvation hath appeared to all men, **teaching** us that, *denying **ungodliness** and **worldly lusts**, we should live soberly, righteously, and godly in the present age, looking for that blessed hope and glorious appearing of our great God and Savior Jesus Christ, who gave Himself for us, that He might redeem us from all iniquity and **purify** unto Himself a peculiar people, zealous of good works."*

Continuing in Romans 12 verse 2 we see that we are not to be *"conformed to this world"*. Doesn't conformed to this world mean that we look just like and act just like the world?

There is another scripture that tells us "To keep ourselves unspotted from the world".

James 1:27
*"Pure religion and undefiled before God and the Father is this, to visit the fatherless and widows in their affliction, and to keep himself **unspotted** from the world."*

Doesn't that sound simple, keep ourselves "unspotted from the world"?

It means "that we are not able to be "spotted" as a worldly person or that we do not have "spots" that look like the world.

Let me ask you, as women professing godliness, does your dress or actions come across as "**looking** like the world" or being "**spotted** as the world"?

God is looking for a heart that is "**honest** and **good**" a "**pure**" heart. We see that Jesus Christ is looking for this type of good ground in Luke 8:15 which says,

*"But that on the good ground are they, which in an **honest and good heart**, having heard the Word, keep it, and bring forth fruit with patience."*

Do you have that honest and good heart that wants to please the Lord in everything you do, body, soul and spirit?

If we plan to please the Lord, we will have to ask Him for an honest and good heart. We will have to desire it more than anything else in our lives, more than pleasing ourselves and more than pleasing others. It will come with a price, the price of a living sacrifice.

In 1 Corinthians 6:18 – 20 NKJV tells us to…

*"Glorify God in our **body** and in our spirit, which are God's"*.

Let's read it…

"Flee sexual immorality. Every sin that a man does is outside the body; but he that commits sexual immorality sins against his own body. Or do you not know that your body is the temple of the Holy Spirit who is in you, whom you have from God, and you are not your own? For you are bought at a price; therefore, glorify God in your body, and in your spirit, which are God's".

We see here that **our body** is not our own. We are bought with a price. When we think of the price that Jesus paid for our salvation doesn't it cause you to realize just how much He does love us?

What do you think that price was?

I believe the price was Jesus coming to the earth, as God in the flesh, living a totally sacrificial life not pleasing Himself but being the servant of all. He was persecuted, abandoned, beaten beyond recognition, suffering mentally, emotionally, and physically in His body, beyond what anyone has ever suffered.

Our bodies (not our spirits or souls) are the temple of the Holy Ghost. Wouldn't this understanding cause us to humbly present our bodies as a living sacrifice (Romans 12:1,2) doing everything we can to bring glory to our Savior and Lord Jesus Christ? Being different in dress, word, and action is not that great of a price when we consider what it cost Jesus to redeem us.

Notes:

"Follow peace with all men, and holiness, *without which no man shall see the Lord:" Hebrews 12:14*

Chapter Ten
What Kind of Attire?

I believe it is very important that we as, women dress in a modest, shamefaced manner so we can please God in our lives. This is so important to God that He tells the elder women to teach the younger women.

We see this in Paul's letter to Titus.

Titus 2:3-5

*"The older women likewise that they be reverent in behavior, not slanderers, not given to much wine, teachers of good things — that they admonish the young women to love their husbands, to love their children, to be **discreet, chaste**, homemakers (keepers at home), good, obedient to their own husbands, that the Word of God may not be **blasphemed**." NKJV*

Wow! This is so important, that the *"Word of God is not blasphemed"*.

Let us look at the words discreet and chaste...

According to Strong's Concordance **discreet** "sophron" G4998 means 1. Safe (sound) in mind, i.e., *self-controlled*.

The dictionary says, 1. **"careful and circumspect** in one's speech or actions, especially in order to avoid offense or to gain an advantage."

Chaste in the concordance means 1. Properly clean, **innocent, modest,** perfect.

The dictionary says, 1. "Abstaining from extra-marital, or from all, sexual intercource."2. "**Not** having any sexual nature or intention".

Do we want to be like the woman in Proverbs 11:22? It says...

"As a jewel of gold in a swine's snout, so is a fair woman which is without discretion."

Shouldn't our attire and actions reflect holiness and godliness? We see a woman without discretion or chastity in Proverbs 7. We should consider ourselves in this. This is very serious...

Proverbs 7:1-27 is written to men, but it is also written to women. Let's start with verse one, it tells men,

> *"My son, keep My words, and treasure my commands within you... Verse five says "That they may **keep you from the immoral woman**, from the seductress who flatters with her words." NKJV*

This is instruction to men to seek after wisdom so that they will recognize an immoral woman as a harlot or prostitute. We notice in verse five that the woman flatters with her words. We know that men are tempted by a woman that flatters with her words.

But let's look further in Verses 6-15:

> *"For at the window of my house I looked through my casement, and beheld among the simple ones, (one without wisdom) I discerned among the youths, a young man void of under-*

*standing, passing through the street **near her corner**; and he went the way to her house, 9. In the twilight in the evening, in the black and dark night: And, behold, there met him a woman with the **attire of an harlot**, and subtil of heart. She is loud and stubborn; her feet abide not in her house: Now is she without, now in the streets, and lies in wait at every corner. So, she caught him, and kissed him, and with an impudent face said unto him, I have peace offerings with me; this day have I paid my vows. Therefore, came I forth to meet thee, diligently to seek your face, and I have found thee.*

In verse 21 we see…

"With her much fair speech she caused him to yield, with the flattering of her lips she forced him.

In verse 26,27 we see…

"For she has cast down many wounded: yea, many strong men have been slain by her. Her

house is the way to hell, going down to the chambers of death."

You may be wondering why I would choose this passage for this study about women's adornment, apparel, their spirits and attitudes.

Let's look at the Scripture in verse 10 it says that there met him a woman with the *"attire of a harlot"*.

We need to ask ourselves what the "attire of a harlot" is?

Don't you think that a harlot is one that seduces (tempts to lust) or attracts a man towards herself by wearing clothes that reveal, especially cleavage, belly and thigh?

We see this in this passage her goal was to cause the man to be so attracted and seduced by her, that he could not resist wanting her. A harlot is one that does not care about others, it is **all** about what she wants for **herself**. She has no love for anyone but herself. We may think, but I don't look like, act like or dress like a harlot. But are you sure? Many of today's fashions are designed to draw attention and accentuate the female body thus drawing the eyes and attention of a man. It is no coincidence that the fashion industry uses words like alluring, brash, bold, sexy, and seductive to describe the latest hot (another deceptive word) fashion trend. I believe their true agenda is really to entice, deceive and seduce women into compromising their morals and common sense thus manipulating them to wear their ungodly garments.

While writing this book and thinking about the fashion industry and how they have influenced the majority of women in this nation to let down their morals and inhibitions, I decided to look up on the Internet to find out who actually invented the miniskirt. I came across information that actually blew me away.

Here is what I found...

This is the title for the article I found in the New York Post. "Mary Quant, '60s designer who invented the miniskirt, dead at 93." This article was published on April 13, 2023. Here is some of the information from this article...

Mary Quant, the British fashion designer who popularized the miniskirt and shaped the 1960s "youthquake," has died. Some people also credited Quant with inventing the miniskirt, which she introduced in London in 1966.

She paired the shocking look with innovative tights and accessories. With her unmistakable blunt bob haircut, the trendsetter also popularized hotpants among youth.

This article says "Quant's design style was sexy and fun-- and distinctly different from floral day dresses that women wore post-World War II.

She catered the miniskirt to a young audience, selecting colors and materials that would appeal to them while also keeping it affordable during the money – cautious time period.

Some of her admirers even compared her impact on fashion to the Beatles influence on music.

But not everyone was impressed by Quant's daringly short styles: in 1967, The Guardian asked whether her clothes could be considered "vulgar." She replied, "Good taste is death, vulgarity is life,"

Quant explained that her models' provocative poses represented the era's sexual openness, which was fueled by the development of the birth control pill. The mini's meteoric rise coincided with the nascent women's movement of the era. Commercial availability of the pill in 1961 encouraged sexual liberation and the miniskirt was the symbol of movement, worn by feminist front-runners such as Germaine Greer and Gloria Steinem.

She opened more Bazaar stores throughout London before exporting her clothes to America, where the "British invasion" was in full swing.

This article tells us quite a bit about the motives and agendas behind the invention of "vulgar" apparel, including the miniskirt and hotpants.

In more research about the invention of the miniskirt I came across more information about Quant in the Guardian article.

It says, her designs sparked a mass market – boom in miniskirts, with hemlines starting just above the knee but steadily creeping upwards. In 1967, she told The Guardian that her shorter dresses and skirts, made in loud colors, were "arrogant, aggressive and sexy".

Despite now being highly praised for liberating British women from restrictive and overly formal clothing, Quant's designs were not accepted by everyone at the time. Although they were all the rage in London, miniskirts were considered "**mad**" in other cities, even in Paris and New York.

Closer to home, Quant recalled in her 1966 memoir Quant by Quant that men would protest against her clothing. "City gents in bowler hats beat on our shop windows with their umbrellas shouting, "**Immoral!**" and "**Disgusting**" at the sight of our miniskirts over tights," she wrote.

She would make provocative statements about sexuality and her private life as well, which perhaps went along with her clothes, which were seen as quite **outrageous** at the time", as per the Fashion Network.

I sure would not want the wealth that this woman and others have from their influence on youth and older women/men. The Bible says in Mark 8:36, 37...

> *"What profit is it if a man gains the whole world and loses his own soul? For what shall a man give in exchange for his soul?"*

Note that Quant paired the miniskirt with tights. Today women wear tights without a skirt over them. (Which was considered underwear not long ago). We have even gotten worse than "immoral and disgusting"!

How has this nation and even the churches gone from total modesty to lewd, seductive, provocative apparel within a century? We see that in the previous article that most people were scandalized and did not like the lewdness of the mini-skirt and hotpants at first. But over time, like a frog in hot water, people have gone from standing against this lewdness, to accepting it and now embracing at, even in the churches.

I'm sure that this is a grief to God, and it is to myself also. It has caused a lot of men to stumble in their walk with the Lord and even go to hell. We see this in the Proverbs when we read about the harlot and her attire.

Do you **dress** and **act** in a manner that attracts or entices men to look at or lust after your body?

I believe that it would be safe to say that a lot of women **DO** dress in a manner that causes men to have a temptation to lust/look at them. You may say that you do not desire men to look/lust after you but God wants to get down to our heart motives. We can understand our motives by thinking about what our thoughts are and by taking note of what we are thinking.

In Proverbs 7 verse 10 it says that the harlot was **subtil** of heart. What does the word **subtil** mean?

The dictionary says that it means 1. **Elusive** 2. **Cunning** 3. **Crafty** 4. **Shrewd.**

We see the same word "subtil" used in Genesis 3:1. This Scripture is talking about the serpent (Satan) who tempted Adam and Eve. We can see why the meaning of "subtil" is cunning, crafty and shrewd. This is the way Satan tempts mankind.

But why would the word "subtil" used regarding Satan be the same word it uses in Proverbs 7:10 about the harlot? In verse 11, we see a description of her. It says, "She is loud and stubborn; her feet abide not in her house: Now is she without, now in the streets, and lies in wait at **every corner**."

This woman in Proverbs 7, the harlot, does not sound like a woman professing godliness, that we see Paul instructing in 1 Timothy 2:9. She sounds like the exact **opposite**.

She is not shamefaced, she is not modest, she is not shy, she is not demure, she is not bashful, in her apparel or in her spirit (attitudes).

She appears to be bold, loud, forward, stubborn, immodest, indecent, lewd, prideful, not sober, subtil (crafty, cunning, and shrewd). We, as women, may not think that we are being like a harlot in our dress and attitudes but is this how we are coming across to men?

When they look at us or interact with us, do they perceive or see us like a harlot, having the spirit of a harlot or do they see God's Holy Spirit?

This is very serious in God's eyes as we see in Proverbs 7 verse 26, 27 that the harlot has...

"cast down many wounded: yes, many strong men have been slain by her. Her house is the way to hell, going down to the chambers of death."

Do we want to be guilty of causing a man, especially Christian men, to give in to their "lust", because of our immodest, indecent, or even lewd dress?

As I said previously, in Matthew 5:28, Jesus said,

*"If a man looks on a woman to lust after her he hath committed adultery **with her** in his heart".*

So, doesn't this take us back to the fact that if we, through our immodest, indecent or even lewd dress cause a man to look on us to lust, that we are guilty of the same things that a harlot does?

Even Jesus said that a man does not have to literally commit adultery with a woman to be guilty and send his soul to hell. He just has to give in to looking and lusting after a woman. This should cause the "fear of God" in our hearts as women. This is very plain and simple.

Again, I will ask you, as women professing godliness, do you believe that you are glorifying God in your body and in your spirit in every way you can, especially in your apparel and actions? Women can dress in modest apparel and still not glorify God in their spirit. Some women just seem to have a seductive, lustful, flirty (attention seeking) attitude toward men. This is the same thing as dressing in an immodest manner.

God wants us to be "holy and pure" in all that we do.

In Hebrews 12:14 it says,

"Follow peace with all men, and holiness, without which no man shall see the Lord:" We see that without "living a holy life" we shall not see the Lord."

We see how God teaches us how His grace causes us to deny ungodliness and worldly lusts.

Titus 2:11-14
*"For the grace of God that bringeth salvation hath appeared to all men, teaching us that, denying **ungodliness** and **worldly lusts**, we should live soberly, righteously, and godly in this present world, looking for that blessed hope and glorious appearing of our great God and Savior Jesus Christ, who gave Himself for us,*

that He might redeem us from all iniquity and **purify** *for Himself His own special people, zealous for good works."*

Earlier we addressed how bad it is for men to lust after women. Jesus made it very severe for them but like I said, it is not just referring to men, because it says in Matthew 5:27-30 that, *"they commit adultery in their heart* **with her**".

I like to compare the lust of men to the lust of women in this way... It is like an electrical outlet... The plug represents a man, the wall receptacle would represent a woman. It takes **both** to complete the circuit.

We, as, women want (in our human nature), a man to **look at us** (lust after us) and see us as attractive or beautiful or maybe even seductive. On the opposite side men want to **look at women** and enjoy/lust after their beauty. So how can we as women blame men for looking or lusting after our bodies if we are by our very dress or lack of it, causing /or attracting/seducing men to desire us?

We are just as **guilty,** according to the Word of God, when we dress in an ungodly seductive manner or act like the harlots of this world.

I asked my husband, who was in the world for some years, what causes a man to struggle in looking/lusting after a woman. He said clothing that is tight, like pants or leggings which accentuates buttocks and pubic area (not too long-ago people called leggings underwear) and /or showing the thigh (above the knee skirts, dresses, or shorts including bike shorts) and low-neck exposing cleavage (be aware while bending over) are a temptation and can cause a man to stumble in his walk with the Lord. I know we do not like to feel like we are being legalistic, but there is an answer to that problem also. My husband's comment was that "Having higher moral standards is not being legalistic". So, keep reading to find out about true "liberty".

Notes:

"For you, brethren, have been called to liberty; only do not use liberty as an opportunity for the flesh, but through love serve one another." Galatians 5:13 NKJV

Chapter Eleven
Liberty in True Beauty

We see in Galatians 5 the issue of legalism being addressed.

I have struggled in this area myself also, wondering if we should even be concerned about how we, as women professing godliness, should dress as long as we are not too extreme in our clothing. But after studying Galatians 5, the Lord seemed to open my eyes to the truth of what is legalism and what is not.

Galatians 5:1
"Stand fast therefore in the liberty wherewith Christ hath made us free and be not entangled again with the yoke of bondage."

I used to think that this meant that we should not be too concerned about the outward appearance, of dress or apparel, as long as we were wearing something that was not extreme. But as I said the more, I studied this passage in Galatians 5, I could see that Paul was saying that if we are trying to be justified by the law (not from a love relationship with Jesus) we are fallen from grace.

> *Galatians 5:3-6*
> *"And I testify again to every man who becomes circumcised that he is a debtor to keep the whole law. You have become estranged from Christ, you who attempt to be justified by law; you have fallen from grace. For we through the spirit eagerly wait for the hope of righteousness by faith. For in Christ Jesus neither circumcision nor circumcision avails anything, but faith working through love." NKJV*

I believe that he is talking about circumcision and the laws of the Old Testament. Paul is not giving Christians an excuse to live in the flesh. (Lewdness and immodesty)

I believe that legalism is trying to obey the Bible in our own strength and in our own flesh. According to the Scriptures and my own experience, when we walk in the Spirit (a close love relationship with Jesus Christ) it is a delight for us to please our Savior and Lord. The commandments that the Word instructs us to do are not grievous but are **life** and **peace** to us. (Romans 8:6-9)

In 1 John 5:3 we see this...

*"For this is the love of God, that we keep His commandments: and His commandments are **not grievous**."*

In Galatians 5, we can see that Paul was **not** talking about our liberty in Christ to "allow walking in the flesh". In verse 13, 14 he makes it very clear...

*"For, you brethren, have been called to liberty; only do not use liberty as an **opportunity** for the **flesh**, but through love serve one another. For all the law is fulfilled in one word, even in this; You shall love your neighbor as yourself."*

In verse 16, it says,

> *"I say then: walk in the Spirit, and you shall* ***not*** *fulfill the* ***lust of the flesh.***" *NKJV*

Would you, as a woman professing godliness, say that when a woman dresses in a provocative, attention getting or seductive way she is "giving occasion to the flesh"? Do you believe that she is in love serving others? I think not. But if we have an honest and good heart wanting to please the Lord with all our heart, we will ask God to show us His way of holiness, godliness and righteousness in how we dress and adorn ourselves.

What I have brought out in the Scripture so far is enough to show God's heart in His desire for us to be His temple, glorifying Him in our bodies and spirits. Do you, my dear friend, want to please the Lord in your life by honoring Him with modest, shamefaced, decent, pure apparel and conduct?

From what I read in the Scripture; God is not pleased with anything else. Will we love God and put Him first or love ourselves and put ourselves first?

Notes:

"Oh, worship the Lord in the beauty of holiness: fear before Him, all the earth." Psalm 96:9

Chapter Twelve
The Beauty of Holiness

This leads me to another subject related to this. Shouldn't we ask ourselves if we are living in the **"fear of God"**? How important is it to walk in the fear of God? It seems to me that from what I have observed in women is a lack of fear of God. Do we even understand what the fear of God is?

There is a scripture in Proverbs 8:13 that says,

> *"The fear of the Lord is to hate evil: pride, and arrogance, and the evil way, and the froward mouth, do I hate."*

And if our immodest apparel and actions are like a harlot, then isn't it **evil** and of the evil way?

Do we have pride in our hearts when we are displaying our sexuality to men? It does not sound like having the "fear of God". I believe that the "fear of God" is when we realize that God **sees** and **knows** everything. He **sees us** dressing in a manner that is seductive, attracting men's attention, and causing men to lust after us. He knows our heart and motives so should we not "fear God"? Maybe many women dress in indecent (immodest, lewd) clothing because they want to be like everyone else, or in other words, not different from the world. But this is also the wrong motive.

We see in Proverbs 29:25 that...

"The fear of man brings a snare: but whoever trusts in the Lord shall be safe." NKJV

If we, as women professing godliness, care more about what other people think about us, than what our God does, then we do have "the fear of man". It says that we cannot fear man and God at the same time, so we must choose who we will serve.

In 2 Corinthians 6:17,18 it says...

"Therefore, come out from among them, and be separate, says the Lord, do not touch what is unclean, and I will receive you. I will be a Father to you, and you shall be My sons and daughters, says the Lord Almighty." NKJV

2 Corinthians 7:1 goes on to say,

"Having therefore these promises, dearly beloved, let us cleanse ourselves from all filthiness of the flesh and spirit, perfecting holiness in the fear of God."

The real question is do we truly want to fear God which should cause us to cleanse ourselves from all **filthiness** of the **flesh** and spirit? Then according to what this passage is saying it sounds like we will have to "come out from among them and be separate and touch not the unclean thing" and that is when God will receive us as His sons and daughters.

This is a truly hard thing for the flesh to submit to God in. We cannot do this in our own selves, we have to cry out for God to help us and to change us. This is not the natural way we as humans are because we want to be accepted by men. Our first and strongest desire should be to "fear God".

If I am reading this passage correctly it seems like it is saying that God does not even receive us as His sons and daughters unless we "come out from among them and be separate".

We see in Matthew 7:13, 14 that Jesus said,

> *"Enter in at the strait gate: for wide is the gate, and broad is the way, that leads to destruction, and many there be which go in thereat: Because strait is the gate, and narrow is the way, which leads onto life, and few there be that find it."*

We see in verse 21 of the same chapter, it says,

> *"Not everyone that says unto Me, Lord, Lord, shall enter into the kingdom of heaven; but he that does the will of My Father which is in heaven."*

What does this say to each and every one of us? Does it sound like it will be easy or that there will be many that will enter this narrow gate? It says that few will find it. Some may say you are getting into legalism by saying these things. But I am only quoting what the Word of God says to us all.

If we are deceived to think that all we need to do is say a prayer and ask God into our heart and then we just go to heaven, then we certainly have not read the Word of God or given heed to it.

James 2:19,20
"You believe that there is one God. You do well. Even the demons believe — and tremble!

But do you want to know, oh foolish man, that faith without works is dead?" NKJV

James 2:24
"You see than that a man is justified by works, and not by faith only." NKJV

In conclusion, my heart, which I feel is God's heart for women, would like to appeal to every woman who desires to be a woman professing godliness…to dress and act accordingly.

Do you feel that your relationship with Jesus Christ is very personal, very intimate? Are you striving to be pleasing to Him in the way you dress, in everything you do and everything you say? Do you have a very strong desire to be the bride of Christ?

If so, this is a very life-changing decision that should be contemplated with an honest and good heart. My hearts prayer is that every woman would search and seek to be as close and intimate as she can with Jesus, letting Him transform her life and give her a true **UNFADED BEAUTY**. A heart that shines with the joy, peace and lasting love that will reflect God's love to the world.

Notes:

In His Presence

by Karen Y. Ranney

Lord Jesus,

In Your presence is joy beyond measure,

At your feet I find the greatest treasure.

There is a peace that passes all understanding,

That restores my soul when life is so demanding.

In Your presence I feel completely accepted,

*By a love that overwhelms my heart and relieves all I
have dreaded.*

In Your presence are pleasures forevermore,

Making me look forward to what you have in store...

For me as Your bride

In You I want to abide,

At Your side.

In Your presence I feel Your gentle embrace,

All my tears are wiped away.

In Your presence I know perfect grace,

That erases any fear I will face.

Your presence draws me to You, my Beloved,

And I will bask eternally knowing I am truly loved,

In Your presence.

Song of Solomon 7:10
"I am my Beloved's and His desire is towards me."

Epilogue

Adorned Beauty

Continue in "The New Proverbs 31 Woman Series" by reading "Adorned Beauty", book 2. It continues the trend of developing a love relationship with Jesus that causes us to learn to be an overcomer in the issues we, as women, deal with every day.

Do you struggle with fear, anxiety, depression and complaining, amongst a myriad of other maladies? The second book in this series, with the help of the Holy Spirit, encourages and shares God's Word to help us, as women, to be overcomers in these trying times we live in.

May God open the eyes of your understanding, through His Word and the Holy Spirit to become the woman of God you were meant to be in all areas of your life. To be well pleasing to Him.

Hope this book is a blessing to each woman who reads it!

Look for Book 2, "Adorned Beauty" and others in the "The New Proverb 31 Woman Series" that will be coming soon. It is the sequel to this book "Unfaded Beauty". It gives more in-depth insight into how to develop a deeper relationship with Jesus, and how, with the help of the Holy Spirit, to take off the old way of life and put on the new.

If interested in any of these books, please email me at:

joyfullynew2015@yahoo.com